Welcome to Inky Whi

Volume 9 in the series

A variety of 30 playful, fanciful and cute illustrations for you to bring to life with colour, and most importantly… relax and enjoy.

I always suggest (and do myself) placing a blank sheet under your work page to protect the illustration beneath from bleed-through of certain pens.

To view pages I have coloured myself from my books, for inspiration, and forthcoming book details, please visit my Amazon author page, my Helenclaireart Facebook page (where I post my colouring tutorials videos!) - all can be found via my website: www.Helenclaireart.co.uk

The series so far:
Inky Ocean, Inky Garden, Inky Mandalas, Inky Mandalas Mix, Inky Extreme, Inky Dinky Blossom, Inky Lifestyle, Inky Galaxy… and now Inky Whimsy.

I hope you find this book lots of fun to colour!

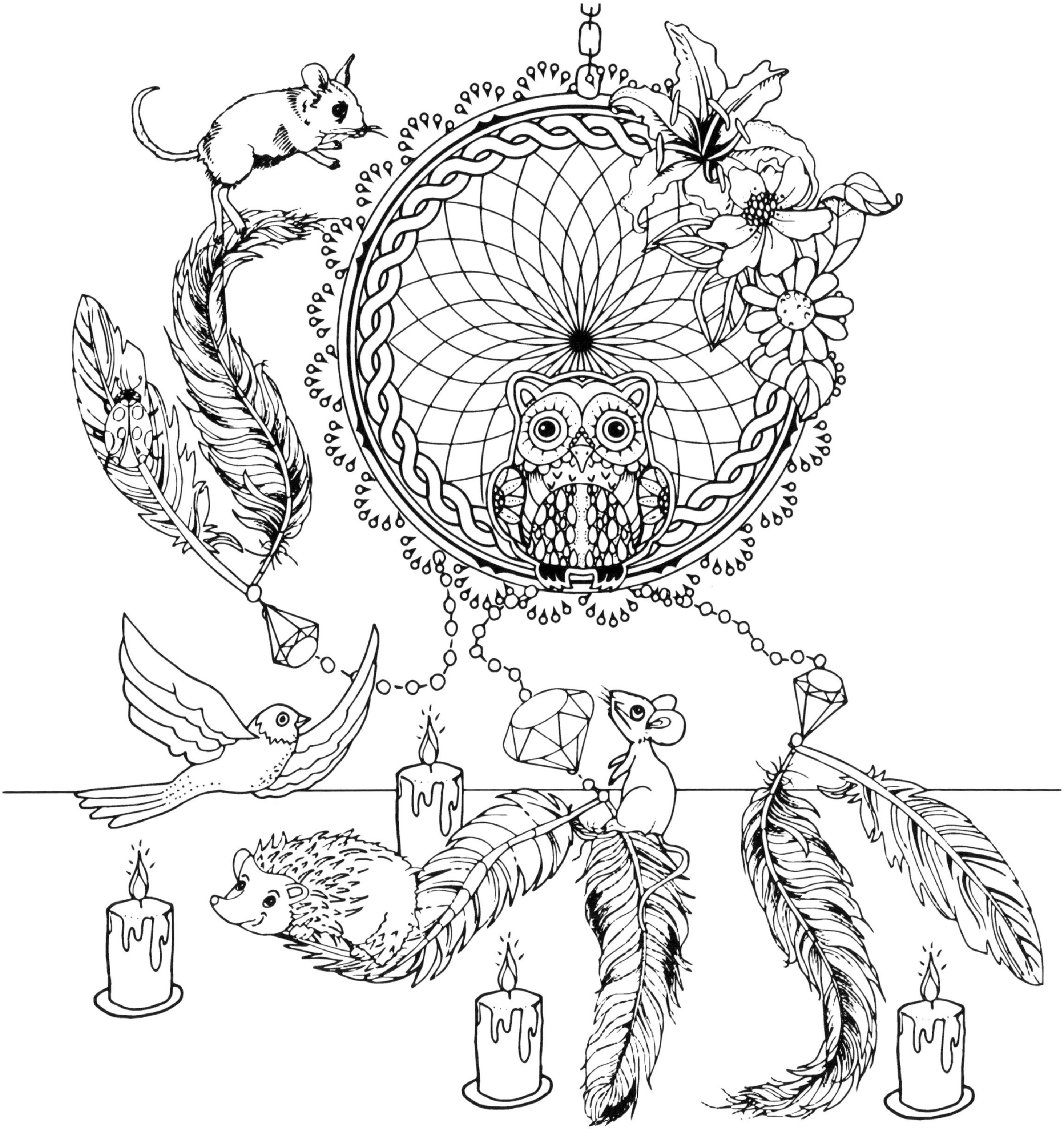

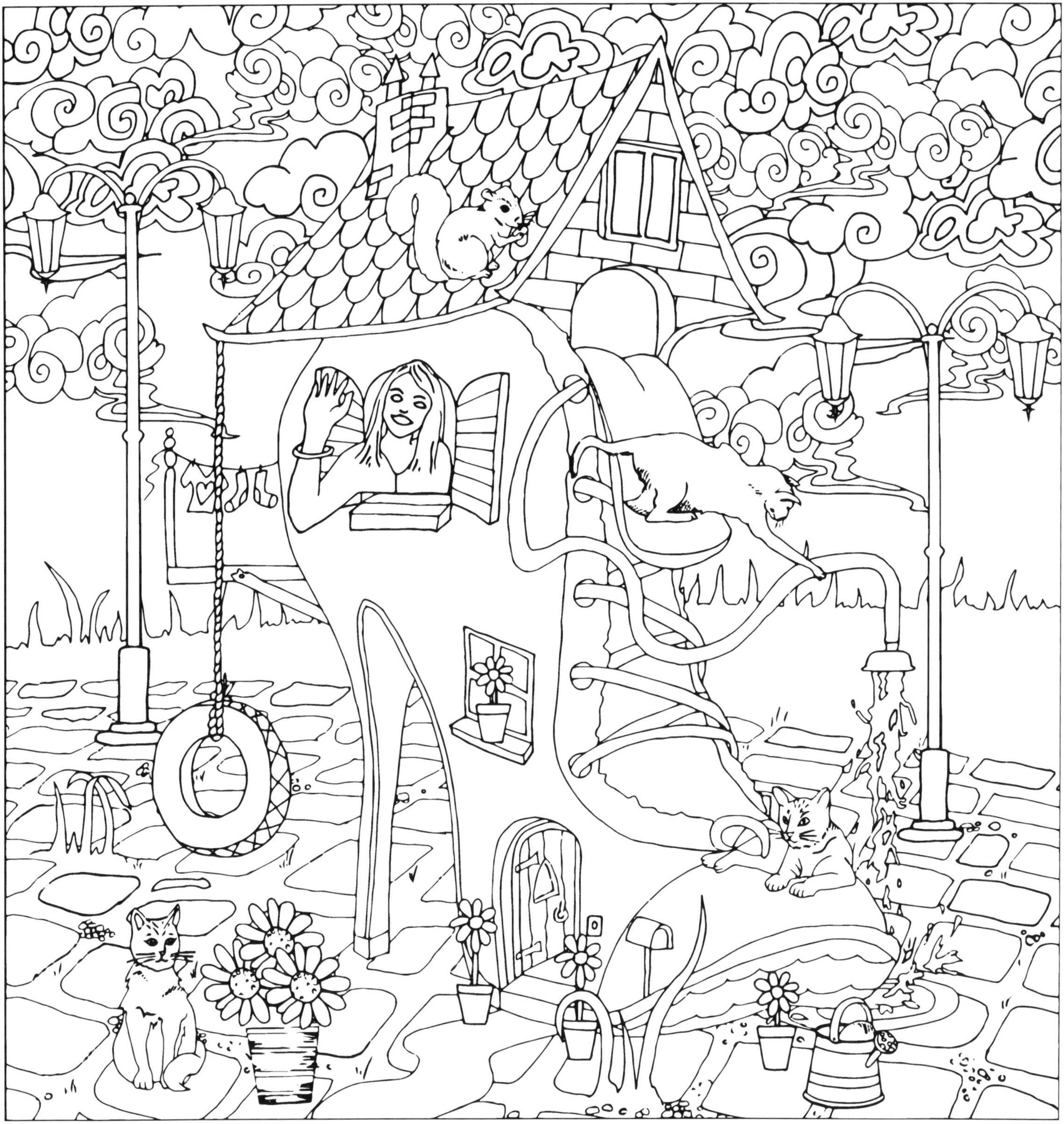